The Toolbox

by

Anne & Harlow Rockwell

COLLIER BOOKS

Division of Macmillan Publishing Co., Inc.

NEW YORK

Macmillan Publishing Co., Inc., 866 Third Avenue, New York, N.Y. 10022
Collier Macmillan Canada Ltd.

Library of Congress catalog card number: 72-119836
The Toolbox is published in a hardcover edition by Macmillan Publishing Co., Inc.
Printed in the United States of America
First Collier Books Edition 1974
ISBN 0-02-044800-7
10 9 8 7 6 5 4 3

For Oliver

In my cellar there is a toolbox.
It is dark brown where hands
have touched it.

It has a saw

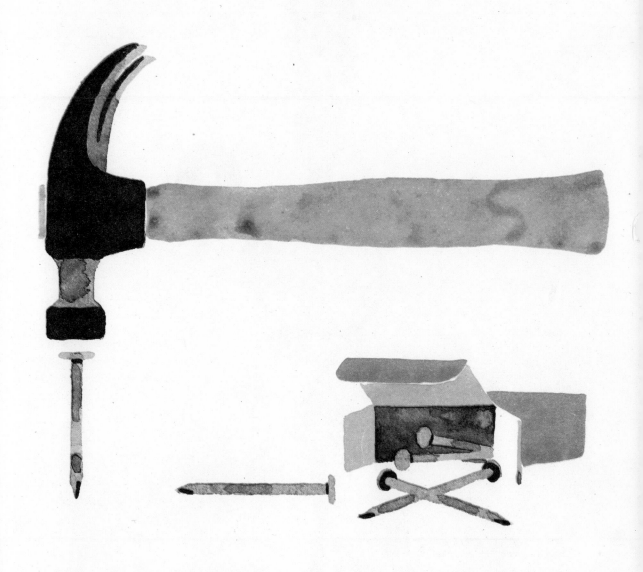

and a hammer and nails,

and a drill
that goes around and around

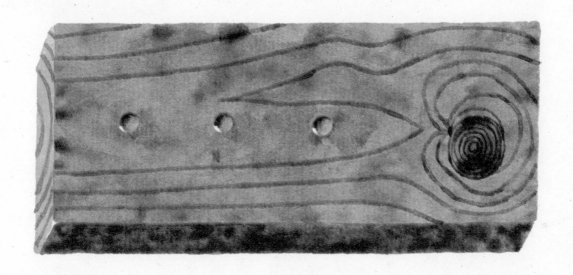

and makes holes in wood.

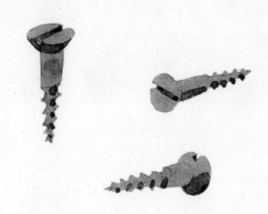

It has screws and a screwdriver,

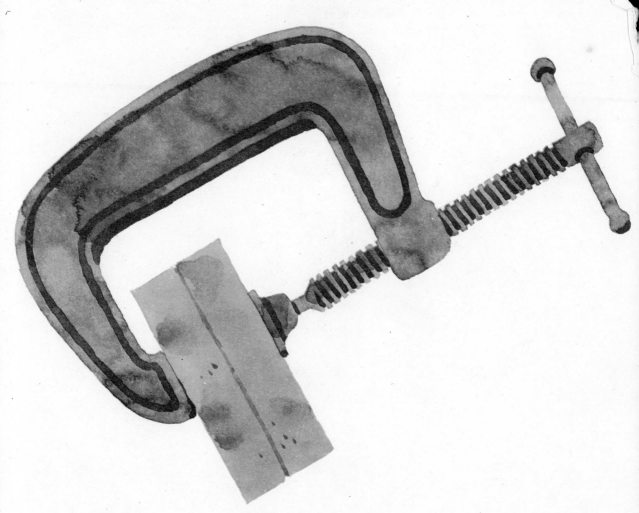

and there is a clamp that holds
pieces of wood together.

There is a big, strong wrench

that turns the big, fat nuts
and bolts,

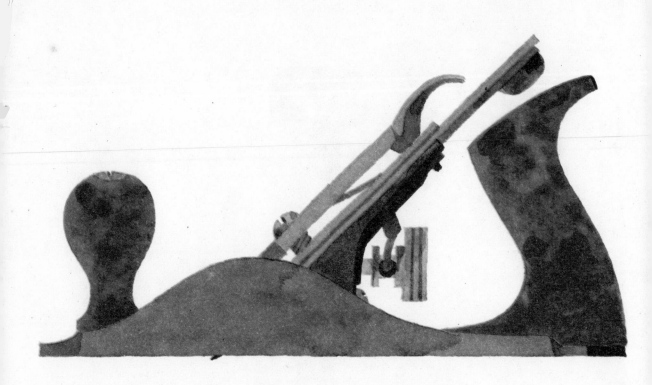

and there is a plane that
smooths wood

and makes curly shavings.

There is a ruler that measures.

There are pliers that pinch.

There is sandpaper to smooth
wood and plaster.

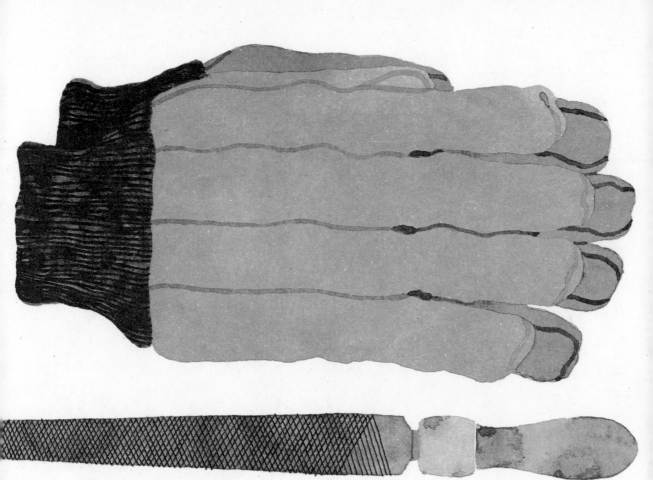

There are work gloves, and there
is a file to rub on rough edges
of metal to make them smooth.

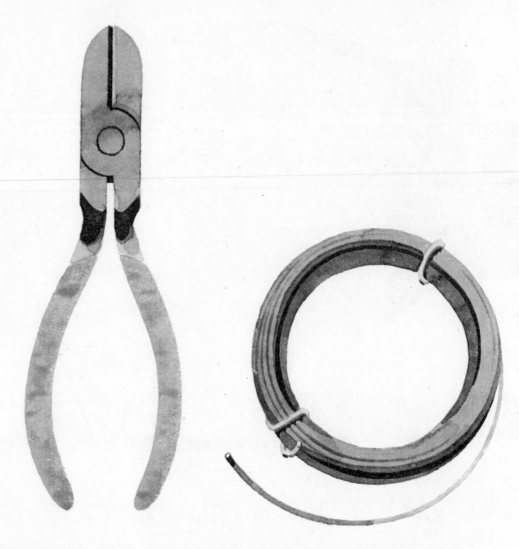

There are sharp wire cutters
and a roll of wire.

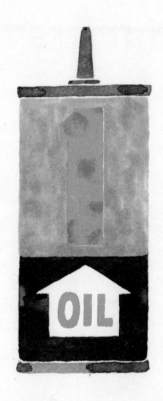

There is an oil can with
a tiny hole.

It is my father's toolbox.